VICTORY (

How to

EAT WELL, LIVE WELL,

PLAN BALANCED MEALS,

under

FOOD RATIONING

British Library Cataloguing-in-Publication Data

A catalogue record for this book is available from
the British Library

CONTENTS

The *Vintage Cookery Books* Series

A Short History of the Cook Book

One might be forgiven for thinking, in our age of celebrity chefs and glossy publications, that cook books are a relatively modern occurrence. However cook books have an incredibly long history, dating as far back as the first century CE.

The oldest collection of recipes that has survived in Europe is *De Re Coquinaria*, written in Latin. An early version was first compiled sometime in the first century and has often been attributed to the Roman gourmet, Marcus Gavius Apicius. An even earlier example (though less recognisable as a modern cook book), was also found in the Roman empire. This was the first known food writer – a Greek Sicilian named Archestratus, who lived in the fourth century BCE. He wrote a poem that spoke of using 'top quality and seasonal' ingredients, and insisted that flavours should not be masked by spices, herbs or other seasonings. Archestratus placed special importance on the simple preparation of fish.

Simplicity was abandoned and replaced by a culture of gastronomy as the Roman Empire developed however. By the time *De Re Coquinaria* was published, it contained 470 recipes calling for heavy use of spices and herbs. After a long interval, the first recipe books to be compiled in Europe since Late Antiquity started to appear in the thirteenth century. About a hundred are known to have survived, some fragmentary, from the age before printing. The earliest genuinely medieval recipes have been found in a Danish manuscript dating from around

◇◇

1300, which in turn is a copy of older texts that date back to the early thirteenth century or perhaps earlier. Chinese cook books have also been found, dating to around this time – and one of the earliest surviving Chinese-language cookbooks; Hu Sihui's *Important Principles of Food and Drink* is believed to have been written in 1330.

German manuscripts are among the most numerous examples of cook books, among them being *The Book of Good Food* written in 1350 and *Kitchen Mastery* written in 1485. Two French collections are probably the most famous: *Le Viandier* ('The Provisioner') which was compiled in the late fourteenth century by Guillaume Tirel, and *The Householder of Paris*; a household book written by an anonymous middle class Parisian in the 1390s. Recipes originating in England include the earliest recorded recipe for ravioli, and the renowned *Forme of Cury* (mid-fourteenth century), compiled by the Master Cooks of King Richard II of England.

Cookbooks that serve as basic kitchen references (sometimes known as 'kitchen bibles') began to appear in the early modern period. They provided not just recipes but overall instructions for both kitchen technique and household management. Such books were written primarily for housewives and occasionally domestic servants, as opposed to professional cooks. Containing a veritable wealth of information, books such as *The Joy of Cooking* (USA), *La Bonne Cuisine de Madame E. Saint-Ange* (France), *The Art of Cookery* (UK), *Il Cucchiaio D'Argento* (Italy), and *A Gift to Young Housewives* (Russia) have served as records for entire national cuisines. With the advent of the printing press in the sixteenth and seventeenth centuries, numerous books were written on how to manage households and prepare food. In Holland and England especially, competition grew between the noble families as to who could prepare the most lavish banquet.

By the 1660s, cookery had progressed to an art form and good cooks were in demand. Many of these professional chefs took full advantage of the new trend, and published their own books detailing their recipes in competition with their rivals. By the nineteenth century, the Victorian preoccupation for domestic respectability brought about the emergence of cookery writing in its modern form. Although eclipsed in fame and regard by Isabella Beeton, the first modern cookery writer and compiler of recipes for the home was Eliza Acton. Her pioneering cookbook, *Modern Cookery for Private Families* (published in 1845), was aimed at the domestic reader rather than the professional cook or chef. This was an immensely influential book, and it established the format for modern writing about cookery.

The publication of *Modern Cookery* introduced the now-universal practice of listing the ingredients and suggested cooking times with each recipe. It also included the first recipe for Brussels sprouts. The book long survived its author, remaining in print until 1914 – functioning as an important influence on Isabella Beeton. Beeton went on to write and publish *Mrs Beeton's Book of Household Management* in twenty-four monthly parts between 1857 and 1861. Of the 1,112 pages detailing domestic issues, over 900 contained recipes, such that another popular name for the volume is *Mrs Beeton's Cookbook*. Most of the recipes were illustrated with coloured engravings, and it was the first book to show recipes in a format that is still used today. In 1896, the American cook Fannie Farmer published her illustrious work, *The Boston Cooking School Cookbook*, which contained some 1,849 recipes.

A good store of vintage cook books should be a kitchen staple for any creative cook. And as such, this series provides a collection of works, designed to instruct, inform and entertain the modern-day reader on times, peoples and foods of the past. Today, the simple pleasures of practical household skills (so wonderfully demonstrated in these books) have been all but forgotten. Now, it's time to get back to basics. This series will take the reader back to the golden age of practical skills; an age where making and mending, cooking and preserving, brewing and bottling, were all done within the home.

The *Vintage Cookery Books* series hopes to bring old wisdom and classic techniques back to life, as we have so much to learn from 'the old ways' of cooking. Not only can these books provide a fascinating window into past societies, cultures and every-day life, but they also let us actively delve into our own history – with a taste of what, how and when, people ate, drank, and socialised. Enjoy.

HOW TO FEED YOUR FAMILY IN WARTIME

SIMPLE RECIPES THAT SAVE RATION POINTS

Healthy eating and healthy living are more important than ever. Every day you read the urgent warning that "Uncle Sam needs us STRONG." It is the patriotic job of every wife and mother to keep her household well, well nourished, well prepared for the strain of extra work and wartime worries. Good food is a vital part of strengthening a nation for war. A healthy home must be a *clean* home, too. That's why the makers of LYSOL Disinfectant offer this timely book for home-makers. The text matter on nutrition, the suggestions for balanced meals, the recipes, have all been prepared by Demetria Taylor, nationally known home economics consultant. The rules for thorough cleaning, the use of a disinfectant in the kitchen, bathroom, sickroom, etc., are by the staff of **LYSOL DISINFECTANT**

ONE-DISH DINNERS . . . HOUSEWIVES WHO WORK

One-dish dinners solve many problems for busy homemakers, whether they work a shift in a war factory, or devote their "spare" time to the Red Gross, A.W.V.S. and other war activities. You see, one-dish dinners save time, save fuel, and save dishwashing. In a single dish, meat, vegetables and an energy food such as potatoes, macaroni, noodles, rice, hominy, or biscuits, are combined. All that is needed to complete an appetizing, "balanced" meal is a first course of soup or tomato juice, a salad, and a simple dessert. Often the last two courses can be combined in a dessert- salad.

One-dish dinners can be cooked in the oven or on top of the stove and usually they can be brought to the table right in the dish in which they were cooked. Often the entire dish can be prepared the night before, stored in the refrigerator and re-heated for dinner the following night.

Every one of the recipes and menus that follow were actually prepared and served by a homemaker who works all day in an airplane factory and cooks dinner for her family at night. She says "I've tried every recipe, with its menu. They are simply grand—such a great help. My husband and sons are delighted with them." Now you try them, won't you?

◇◇

MEAT AND VEGETABLE PIE
6 portions

- 2 cups diced asparagus, cooked or canned
- 2 cups cubed, cooked meat
- 2 cups drained peas, cooked or canned
- 2 cups bouillon gravy*
- 1 1/2 cups biscuit mix

Arrange alternate layers of asparagus, meat and peas in a casserole. Pour gravy into casserole. Cover and chill in refrigerator until ready to serve. Prepare biscuit mix according to directions on the package, roll out 1/2 inch thick on floured board and cut with biscuit cutter. Arrange biscuits on casserole. Bake in a hot oven (450° F.) 15-18 minutes, or until biscuits are brown.

(Start the meal with chilled tomato juice. With the casserole serve raw carrot strips. End with a fruited gelatine dessert and coffee or tea.)

*BOUILLON GRAVY
6 portions

- 4 tablespoons fat
- 2 tablespoons minced onion
- 4 tablespoons flour
- 2 bouillon cubes, plus 2 cups water
- Salt and pepper

Melt fat; add onion and cook over low heat until onion is soft but not brown. Add flour; blend. Add bouillon, and cook, stirring constantly, until thickened. Season to taste with salt and pepper. (Left-over gravy may be added if desired.)

◇◇◇

FRANKFURTER CASSEROLE
6 portions

- 1 (9-oz.) package elbow macaroni
- 1 1/2 cups grated American cheddar cheese
- 1 tall can evaporated milk

- 1 1/2 teaspoons salt
- few grains pepper
- 2 cups drained green beans, cooked or canned
- 1 pound frankfurters, sliced

Cook macaroni in boiling salted water until tender; drain; rinse with hot water. Combine macaroni, cheese, evaporated milk, salt and pepper. Add green beans and frankfurter slices; mix well. Pour into large casserole. Cover and chill in refrigerator until ready to serve. Bake in moderate oven (350° F.) 30-40 minutes.

(With the casserole serve tomato and romaine salad. End with a sweet from the bakery and coffee.)

LAMB CURRY EN CASSEROLE
6 portions

- 2 cups cubed, cooked lamb
- 2 1/2 cups cooked rice
- 2 cups drained peas, cooked or canned

- 1/2 cup seedless raisins
- 2 cups curry sauce*
- 2/3 cup buttered crumbs

Arrange alternate layers of lamb, rice, peas and raisins in a casserole. Pour curry sauce into casserole. Top with buttered crumbs. Cover and chill in refrigerator until ready to serve. Bake in a hot oven (400° F.) 15-20 minutes or until crumbs are brown.

◇◇◇

(Start with pineapple juice. With the casserole serve home-made chutney or relish, and a salad of mixed greens. End with fresh fruit, crackers and cheese.)

*CURRY SAUCE
6 portions

- 4 tablespoons fat
- 4 tablespoons flour
- 1/2 teaspoon salt

- 2 teaspoons curry powder
- 2 cups bouillon or consommé

Melt fat. Combine flour, salt and curry powder; add to fat; blend. Add bouillon or consomme; cook, stirring constantly, until thickened.

SOUPS . . . FULL OF VIM
VIGOR AND VITAMINS

There are lots of tricks with soups that thrifty housewives should know, especially in wartime, when waste is sabotage. The peasant housewives of pre-war Europe knew all these tricks. The soup kettle was their mainstay. Into it went all the odds and ends that extravagant Americans threw away . . . bones, bits of meat, vegetable parings, carrot tops, beet tops, left-overs . . . out of it came a steaming, savory, mouth-watering soup that took first place on the menu.

Now that you are "spending" your ration cards for *ounces* of food, you can't afford to waste. The liquid in a can of vegetables, for example weighs in with the solid food. Into the soup kettle with it! Save what little water remains from home-cooked vegetables for the soup-pot, too. You buy bones with your meat . . . don't waste them . . . drop them into the soup. There's a little dab of corn, a few string beans or a handful of peas left-over . . . drop them in the kettle, too. Buy a nickel's worth of soup greens when you go to market for fresh vegetables . . . you'll get much more than a nickel's worth of flavor in the soup.

Don't forget dried legumes . . . split peas, beans of all kinds, lentils . . . they are rich in food value, hearty and healthy . . . a fine basis for delicious, nourishing soup that sticks to the ribs. Here goes . . . try these recipes in your soup kettle!

OX-TAIL SOUP
6 portions

- 1 oxtail
- seasoned flour
- 2 tablespoons fat
- 2 cups water
- 1/2 teaspoon salt
- 1/8 teaspoon pepper
- 1/8 teaspoon cayenne
- 4 allspice berries
- 1 quart bouillon (made with bouillon cubes)
- 1/2 teaspoon Worcestershire sauce

Wash oxtail; cut in small pieces; roll in seasoned flour; brown in fat in deep saucepan. Add water and seasonings; boil 10 minutes. Skim. Cover and simmer 2-3 hours or until meat is tender. Strain; saving stock. Remove meat from bones; return meat to stock. Add vegetables and bouillon; bring to a boil; simmer 1/2 hour. Add Worcestershire sauce.

LIVER SOUP
6 portions

- 1/2 pound liver, chopped
- 1 cup chopped mushrooms
- 2 teaspoons chopped parsley
- 3 tablespoons fat
- 1 teaspoon salt
- 1/4 teaspoon pepper
- 1/4 teaspoon chili powder
- 1 quart bouillon (made from bouillon cubes)
- 1 tablespoon cornstarch
- cold water
- 1 cup light cream

Cook liver, mushrooms and parsley in fat until lightly browned. Add seasonings and bouillon; cover and simmer 20 minutes. Mix cornstarch to a thin paste with cold water; add a little of the hot soup mixture; blend; stir into remaining hot soup; add cream and simmer 5 minutes, stirring often.

BLACK BEAN SOUP
6 portions

- 1 1/2 cups black beans
- 6 cups cold water
- 1 medium onion, sliced
- 3 tablespoons fat
- celery tops
- marrow bone
- 1/2 teaspoon salt
- 1/4 teaspoon dry mustard
- dash of cayenne
- 1 tablespoon flour
- 6 slices lemon

Soak beans overnight in cold water. Drain; measure water; add enough cold water to make 6 cups (or 3 cups, for smaller recipe); add to beans. Cook onion in 1 tablespoon fat until lightly browned; add to beans with celery tops and bone. Bring to a boil; cover; simmer 3 hours or until beans are soft, adding more water as it cooks away. Remove bones and celery tops; rub soup through a fine sieve. Add seasonings; re-heat. Melt remaining fat; blend in flour; add hot soup gradually. Cook 3 minutes, stirring constantly. Garnish with thin lemon slices. If desired, add 2 tablespoons dry sherry just before serving.

SPLIT PEA OR LENTIL SOUP
6 portions

- 1 cup split peas or lentils
- 6 cups water
- Ham bone or marrow bone
- 1 medium onion, sliced
- 2 cups cooked or canned
- tomatoes
- 1 bayleaf
- 1 teaspoon salt
- 1/8 teaspoon pepper

Soak split peas overnight in cold water. Drain; measure water; add enough cold water to make 6 cups (or 3 cups, if smaller recipe is used); add to split peas. Add bone, onion, tomatoes, bayleaf, salt and pepper. Cover; simmer 2-3 hours or until peas are soft, adding more water as it cooks away. Remove bone; rub soup through a fine sieve. Serve piping hot with toast croûtons.

MAIN DISHES THAT
SPARE RATION COUPONS

Wartime restrictions may prove to be a blessing in disguise. We're going to learn many things about food that will stand us in good stead all our lives. Meats that are unfamiliar now will become tried and true favorites. Ever eat rabbit? Take our word for it—it's good eating. You don't care for liver or kidney? Perhaps you've never had them cooked as they should be. How about oxtail? French chefs consider it a delicacy de luxe . . . and so will you. Beef heart, stuffed with a savory dressing, takes its place proudly as the *piece de resistance* of a "heartening" meal! Tongue was ever a treat—but try it with Gingersnap Gravy for an extra special dinner. Who says this isn't a land of plenty? No need to worry about getting enough body-building protein if you learn your way about!

KIDNEY STEW
6 portions

- 3 beef kidneys or 6 veal kidneys
- 3 tablespoons fat
- 4 tablespoons flour
- 2 cups water
- 1 tablespoon minced onion
- 1/2 teaspoon salt
- 1/8 teaspoon pepper
- 2 cups cooked sliced carrots
- 3 cups hot cooked rice

Split kidneys; remove core, skin and hard membrane; cut into sections. Soak in cold salt water to cover 1 hour; drain. Cook in fat about 3 minutes; add flour; cook until well browned, stirring constantly. Add water, onion, salt and pepper; cover, simmer 15 minutes. Add carrots; heat thoroughly. Serve on rice, or in rice ring.

RABBIT WITH SOUR CREAM GRAVY
6 portions

- 1 rabbit (3 lbs.)
- seasoned flour
- 4 tablespoons fat
- 2 large onions sliced

Have rabbit dressed and cut in serving size pieces. Wash pieces; dredge with seasoned flour. Cook in fat until well-browned on all sides. Remove from pan. Cook onions in fat in pan until soft and browned. Remove onion; replace rabbit; cover with onions. Add salt, pepper and enough boiling water to cover. Add sour cream; cover and simmer 45 minutes or until rabbit is tender.

TONGUE WITH GINGERSNAP GRAVY
6 portions

- 1 fresh beef tongue
- 6 gingersnaps, crushed
- 1/4 cup seedless raisins
- 1/3 cup brown sugar
- 1 cup hot water
- 1/4 cup lemon juice

Scrub tongue; cover with boiling water; bring to boil; skim; simmer, covered until tender (3-4 hours for beef tongue, 2-3 hours for veal tongue). Remove skin and root ends. Combine remaining ingredients; bring to a boil; simmer 15 minutes; serve with tongue.

LIVER AND VEGETABLE CASSEROLE
6 portions

- 3 strips bacon, diced
- 1 cup sliced okra
- 1 cup shelled lima beans
- 1 cup diced celery
- 1 green pepper, diced
- 1 small onion, chopped
- 2 tart apples, sliced
- 1 pound veal or lamb livers, sliced
- 1/2 teaspoon salt
- 1/8 teaspoon pepper
- 2 cups bouillon
- currant jelly

Fry bacon until crisp. (If not available, substitute 3 tablespoons fat.) Add vegetables, apple, liver, seasonings and bouillon; bring to a boil. Pour into casserole; cover; bake in slow oven (300° F.) 1 1/2 hours. Garnish with cubes of jelly just before serving.

BRAISED OXTAIL
6 portions

- 1 oxtail
- seasoned flour
- 1/4 cup fat
- 1 cup water
- 1 cup tomato juice
- 1 teaspoon salt
- 1/8 teaspoon pepper
- 4 allspice berries
- 1 bayleaf
- 4 carrots, sliced
- 1 large onion, chopped
- 1 garlic clove, mashed
- 1/3 cup lemon juice

Cut oxtail in 2-inch pieces; roll in seasoned flour; cook in 2 tablespoons fat until well-browned. Add water, tomato juice and seasonings; bring to a boil; simmer, covered, 3 hours or until tender. Cook carrots, onion and garlic in remaining fat until lightly browned; add to meat; cook 1/2 hour longer. Add lemon juice. Serve at once.

⟡⟡⟡⟡⟡⟡⟡⟡⟡⟡⟡⟡⟡⟡⟡⟡⟡⟡⟡⟡⟡⟡⟡⟡⟡⟡⟡⟡⟡⟡⟡⟡⟡⟡⟡⟡⟡⟡

STUFFED BEEF HEART

Remove veins and arteries from heart; wash thoroughly. Stuff with following mixture: Cook 1 small onion, minced, 3 tablespoons chopped celery, 2 tablespoons minced green pepper in 1 1/2 tablespoons fat until soft. Add 3/4 cup fine, soft bread crumbs, salt, pepper, 1/4 teaspoon poultry seasoning and 1 small carrot grated; mix well. Roll stuffed heart in seasoned flour; brown in hot fat; place in deep casserole. Pour 1 cup water into pan in which heart was browned, bring to a boil; pour into casserole. Add enough more boiling water to half cover heart. Cover; bake in moderate oven (350° F.) 2 hours or until tender. Thicken gravy.

MAKING MEAT RATIONS S-T-R-E-T-C-H

A wartime paradox—the largest supply of meat in history, but less than ever before for American families! The reason? Fighting men need plenty of meat—soldiers, sailors and marines under our own flag and the flags of our fighting allies. Huge quantities must go to them, and we must learn to s-t-r-e-t-c-h what remains. And gladly, too. How? By planning ahead, by learning all about meat cuts, by cooking meat properly with low heat and less water to avoid undue shrinkage, by using every bit, even the trimmings and bones for soup, by ingenuity in using left-overs, by stretching the flavor of meat through combining it with vegetables, bread crumbs, cereals, rice, macaroni, spaghetti, noodles, etc.

The American housewife has never yet fallen down on her job, and she won't this time, either. Meat is an essential food, rich in protein, iron, phosphorus and vitamins. Your family will have enough if you plan carefully, buy wisely and don't waste. Here are some recipes to help:

MEAT BALLS IN GRAVY
6 portions

- 1 1/2 pounds hamburger
- 1/4 cup grated onion
- 1 1/2 teaspoons salt
- 1/4 teaspoon pepper
- 1 egg
- 6 slices dry toast
- 3 tablespoons meat drippings
- 3 tablespoons flour
- 1 1/2 cups milk

Combine meat, onion, salt, pepper and egg; mix well. Cover toast with water; soak thoroughly; squeeze out water; add toast to meat. Shape into balls; brown in drippings. Remove meat. Add flour to fat in pan; blend. Add milk gradually; stir over low heat until smooth and thickened. Add meat balls; cover; simmer 15 minutes.

SPICED MEAT BALLS
6 portions

- 1 pound hamburger
- 1 egg
- 1 cup bread crumbs
- 2 tablespoons chopped fresh
  mint
- 1/2 cup milk
- 1/2 teaspoon cinnamon
- 1 teaspoon salt

Combine all ingredients; mix well. Let stand 10 minutes. Form into cakes. Brown on both sides in a little hot fat. Lower heat and cook 10 minutes, turning once.

STUFFED FLANK STEAK

Combine 1 1/2 cups stale bread crumbs, 2 tablespoons melted butter, 1/4 cup chopped seeded raisins, 1/2 cup broken walnut meats, 1/2 teaspoon salt, few grains pepper; 1/2 teaspoon poultry seasoning; mix well. Spread on flank steak: roll up and tie securely. Brown on all sides in hot fat. Add 1 1/2 cups hot water; cover. Bake in very moderate oven (325° F.) about 2 hours or until tender. Thicken gravy.

LAMB CROQUETTES
6 portions

- 3 cups ground, cooked lamb
- 3/4 teaspoon salt
- 1/2 teaspoon paprika
- 1/8 teaspoon pepper
- 1 1/2 cups thick white sauce
- 1 tablespoon grated onion
- currant jelly
- 1 egg, slightly beaten
- 1 cup fine dry crumbs

Combine lamb, seasonings, white sauce and onion; mix well. Form into 12 rolls or cones with a cube of currant jelly in center of each. Dip in crumbs, then in egg, then in crumbs again. Fry in shallow fat (1 1/2 inches deep) heated to 390° F. for 2 minutes or until golden brown. Serve with mushroom sauce.

BEEF FRITTERS
6 portions

- 2 cups sifted flour
- 2 teaspoons baking powder
- 1 teaspoon salt
- 2 teaspoons sugar
- 1 egg, beaten
- 1 1/2 cups milk
- 1 cup diced cooked beef
- 2 slices crisp bacon, diced (optional)
- 1 tablespoon minced celery

Mix and sift flour, baking powder, salt and sugar. Combine egg and milk; stir into dry ingredients slowly, beating until smooth. Add meat, bacon and celery.-Drop from tablespoons into hot shallow fat (1 1/2 inches deep) heated to 375° F. Fry 2-3 minutes, or until golden brown.

HOT POT
6 portions

- 1 1/2 pounds stewing lamb
- seasoned flour
- 1 1/2 tablespoons fat
- 4 cups water
- 12 small onions
- 12 small potatoes
- 1/2 teaspoon salt
- 1/8 teaspoon pepper
- 2 tablespoons fat
- 2 tablespoons flour

Cut lamb in 1-inch cubes; dust with seasoned flour and brown in fat. Add water, onions, potatoes, salt and pepper. Cover and simmer 1 hour or until vegetables and meat are tender. Arrange meat and vegetables on a platter. Garnish with parsley. Thicken, gravy with remaining fat and flour. Serve separately.

FISH DISHES THAT HAVE RATION POINTS

Once or twice or thrice a week let fish grace your table. Think highly of it, for fish is a nutritious food, rich in protein, minerals and vitamins. Properly cooked, it is fare fit for the gourmet. Seasonings and sauces add a fillip . . . herbs are the thing with fish . . . spice and vinegar play their part. Don't be content with a frying pan . . . try a casserole . . . or ramekins . . . or a steamer. Put on your chef's high hat and go to it! First of all, learn to make Court Bouillon—it's the basis of fine fish cookery.

CAPE COD FISH CHOWDER
6 portions

- 4 pounds cod or haddock
- 4 cups water
- 2 thin slices fat salt pork, diced
- 2 large onions, sliced
- 4 cups sliced raw potatoes
- 4 cups milk
- salt and pepper
- 3 tablespoons butter (optional)

Boil fish 20 minutes in 2 cups water. Fry salt pork in deep kettle. Add onions; cook until soft. Add potatoes and 2 cups boiling water. Drain fish, add liquor to kettle. Simmer until potatoes are tender. Remove skin and bones from fish, do not break up more than is necessary. Add fish to kettle. Simmer 10 minutes. Add milk; bring to scalding point; add salt and pepper to taste. Add butter if desired. Serve with Boston crackers or pilot crackers.

◇◇

CODFISH COTTAGE STYLE
6 portions

- 1 codfish (3 pounds)
- 2 carrots, thinly sliced
- 2 medium onions, minced
- 2 tablespoons butter or
  margarine
- 1 tablespoon chopped parsley
- 1 teaspoon salt
- few grains pepper
- 1/3 cup white wine
- 1 cup white sauce

Split and bone codfish. Cut in serving size pieces. Cook carrots and onions 10 minutes in just enough water to prevent scorching; drain (save any liquid). Place vegetables in saucepan with butter, parsley and fish. Add salt, pepper, white wine and liquid from vegetables. Cover and cook 20 minutes, or until fish is done. Remove fish and vegetables. Boil liquid left in pan, until reduced by one-half. Add white sauce. Season if necessary. Pour over fish and vegetables.

STUFFED BAKED FISH FILLETS
6 portions

- 1 cup chopped onions
- 3 tablespoons fat
- 1/2 cup finely chopped walnuts
- 2 cups cooked rice
- 1/4 teaspoon chili powder
- 1/8 teaspoon pepper
- 1/2 teaspoon salt
- 6 fish fillets
- 2 tablespoons butter
- 1 cup water

Cook onions in fat until soft and yellow; add walnuts, rice, chili powder, pepper and salt; mix well. Spread rice mixture on half of the fillets. Top with remaining fillets; tie securely with string. Place in baking dish; dot with butter. Pour 1 cup water into baking dish. Bake in a moderate oven (350° F.) 30 minutes.

FISH FILLETS CREOLE
6 portions

- 1 tablespoon fat
- 2 tablespoons flour
- 2 sprigs each fresh thyme, parsley and marjoram
- 1/2 teaspoon allspice
- 2 bayleaves
- 1 large onion, minced
- 1 garlic clove, minced
- 6 large tomatoes, chopped
- 1 cup water
- salt and pepper
- 6 thin fish fillets
- 1 lemon, juice

Melt fat, add flour; blend. Chop thyme, parsley and marjoram; add with allspice, bay leaves, onion, garlic, tomatoes and water. Let come to a full boil. Boil 5 minutes. Season to taste with salt and pepper. Add fish fillets and lemon juice. Cover and simmer 15 minutes or until fish is done.

COURT BOUILLON

- 1/4 cup chopped carrots
- 1/4 cup chopped onion
- 1/4 cup chopped celery
- 1 sprig parsley
- 1 tablespoon fat
- 1 1/2 quarts water

Cook vegetables and parsley in fat 3 minutes; place in kettle. Add remaining ingredients; cover and heat slowly to boiling; simmer 5 minutes, Use for boiling fish.

EGGS ARE GOOD MEAT SUBSTITUTES

Eggs are a perfect meat substitute, and at seasons when the price comes down, we should take advantage of this nutritious note, and serve egg main dishes now and again. But an egg gives us more than protein . . . it holds every one of the vitamins as well as three important minerals . . . calcium, phosphorus and iron.

Don't let the color of the shell distract you . . . it has nothing at all to do with food value. So, buy brown or white, whichever is less expensive, as long as freshness is assured.

Cook eggs at low temperatures no matter what the method. *Never boil them.* Keep the water just below the boiling point and the eggs will be easy to digest.

The nutrition rule is "eat at least three or four eggs a week—better still, one a day." Count eggs used in cooking as well as those consumed "as is". But count 'em . . . and eat 'em.

PEASANT OMELET
6 portions

- 6 eggs
- 6 tablespoons water
- 1 teaspoon salt
- 1/8 teaspoon pepper
- 1 cup finely diced cooked potatoes
- 4 tablespoons fat

Beat eggs slightly; add water, salt and pepper. Cook potatoes in 2 tablespoons fat until golden brown; add to egg mixture. Melt remaining fat in frying pan. Turn egg mixture into frying pan. Cook over moderate heat. As it cooks, lift edges toward center and tip pan so that uncooked portion flows under cooked portion. When brown on the bottom, fold over and serve at once.

EGGS IN RICE NESTS
6 portions

- 3 cups hot cooked rice
- 1/2 cup grated cheese
- 6 eggs
- salt, pepper, paprika

Fill ramekins with rice, making a hollow. Drop an egg in each hollow. Sprinkle rice with grated cheese. Sprinkle eggs with salt, pepper and paprika. Bake in a moderate oven (350° F.) until eggs are set.

EGGS MARGUERITE
6 portions

- 6 baked Idaho potatoes
- 3 cups creamed vegetables
- 6 poached eggs
- 1/2 cup grated American cheddar cheese

Scoop all pulp from potatoes; mash; season. Fill shells with creamed vegetables. Make a border of mashed potato; place poached egg on top of creamed vegetables. Sprinkle egg with cheese. Place in a moderate oven (350° F.) until cheese melts and browns.

EGGS TIA JUANA
6 portions

- 6 large tomatoes
- 2 tablespoons minced green pepper
- 1/2 cup water
- 1/4 teaspoon salt
- few grains pepper
- 1/4 teaspoon chili powder
- 6 eggs
- Worcestershire sauce

Wash tomatoes; remove stem ends: Scoop out a hollow deep enough to hold an egg. Chop pulp that is removed; add green pepper, water, salt, pepper and chili powder; pour into baking dish. Sprinkle tomatoes with salt and pepper; place in baking dish. Bake in a moderately hot oven (375° F.) 10 minutes. Remove from oven. Drop an egg in hollow of each tomato. Return to oven; bake 15 minutes or until eggs are set. Dash a little Worcestershire sauce on each egg. Serve at once, with the sauce in the pan.

DUTCH TREAT

Make a large, plain omelet. Meanwhile prepare a cheese sauce as follows: melt 1/2 pound processed American cheese over hot water; stir in 1/3 cup milk; add 2 tablespoons finely cut chives. Remove omelet to a hot platter; cover with cheese sauce; fold over. Serve at once.

CURRIED EGGS AND MUSHROOMS
6 portions

- 6 tablespoons fat
- 6 tablespoons flour
- 1/2 teaspoon salt
- 1-2 teaspoons curry powder

◇◇◇

- 1/2 teaspoon paprika
- 3 cups bouillon
- 1/2 pound mushrooms, sliced
- 6 hard-cooked eggs, sliced

Melt fat; mix flour, salt, curry powder and paprika; blend with fat. Add bouillon. Cook over low heat, stirring constantly until thickened. Cover and simmer 10 minutes. Meanwhile cook mushrooms in a little fat until golden brown. Add with eggs to curry sauce. Serve with rice, noodles or on toast.

ORIENTAL OMELET
6 portions

- 1 garlic clove, minced
- 2 tablespoons fat
- 1/2 pound ground pork
- 1/4 cup finely chopped peanuts
- 1/3 cup minced onion
- 2 teaspoons sugar
- 1 teaspoon Worcestershire sauce
- 1/8 teaspoon pepper
- 6 eggs, beaten

Fry garlic in 1 tablespoon fat. Add pork, peanuts and onions; cook slowly until meat is done. Add sugar, Worcestershire sauce and pepper and mix well. Remove from heat. Make eggs into plain omelet. Spread with pork mixture; roll up. Serve with tomato sauce if desired.

GET ACQUAINTED WITH SOYA BEANS AND PEANUTS

Meet two strange, unique vegetables. They belong to the legume family and their names are Soya Beans and Peanuts. Oh, yes, peanuts *are* vegetables . . . science tells us so. Maybe you think this fact is unique enough, but that wasn't what we meant. These two legumes are the *only* vegetables that are real meat substitutes. They supply us with complete body-building proteins. Now isn't that good news in these days of meat shortages?

The soya bean crop this year is expected to be tremendous. And the native peanut (and peanut butter!) will be with us in abundance. So it is up to us to make good use of both. Here are some grand recipes to help.

BAKED SOYA BEANS
6 portions

- 3 cups soya beans
- 1 medium onion
- 1/4 pound fat salt pork
- 1 1/2 teaspoons salt
- 1/3 cup dark molasses
- 1/2 teaspoon dry mustard
- 1/2 teaspoon Worcestershire sauce
- Boiling water

Wash beans; soak in cold water overnight; drain. Cover with fresh water; simmer 2-3 hours or until nearly tender. Put the onion in a bean pot or deep casserole. Turn beans into bean pot. Pour boiling water over pork; scrape rind until white; score

◇◇

in 1/2-inch strips and press into top of beans, leaving only rind exposed. Mix salt, molasses, mustard and Worcestershire sauce; add enough boiling water to cover beans. Cover bean pot and bake in a slow oven (300° F.) 6 hours, adding more water if necessary to keep beans just covered Remove cover of bean pot during last half hour of baking to brown pork and beans.

PEANUT-HONEY PUDDING
6 portions

- 2 cups milk, scalded
- 1 cup soft bread crumbs
- 1/2 cup evaporated milk
- 1/2 cup peanut butter
- 1/4 cup honey
- 1/4 teaspoon salt
- 1/4 teaspoon ginger
- 1 egg, slightly beaten

Combine milk and crumbs; let stand 15 minutes. Add half of evaporated milk to peanut butter; beat smooth. Add remaining milk, beat smooth. Mix honey, salt and ginger; add to peanut butter mixture. Combine crumb mixture and peanut butter mixture. Add egg; mix well. Pour into casserole; set in pan of warm water. Bake in a moderate oven (350° F.) 1 1/2 hours or until inserted knife comes out clean.

PEANUT BISQUE
6 portions

- 6 tablespoons peanut butter
- 1 can condensed green pea soup
- 3 tablespoons flour
- 2 1/2 cups milk

Heat peanut butter; blend in flour. Add combined soup and milk. Cook over hot water, stirring constantly until thickened. Cover; cook 10 minutes longer.

CHILI CON CARNE
6 portions

- 1/4 pound salt pork, diced
- 1/3 cup chopped onions
- 3 cups cooked or canned tomatoes
- 1 pound hamburger
- 1 tablespoon chili powder
- 3 cups cooked soya beans

Fry salt pork until crisp. Remove pork; brown the onions in fat in pan. Add hamburger; cook slowly, stirring often, until browned. Add pork and remaining ingredients. Simmer 30 minutes.

SUNDAY NIGHT SANDWICHES

Mash cooked soya beans; add chili sauce to taste. Spread on slices of hot toast. Top with boned domestic sardines and another slice of toast. Serve hot.

SOYA BEAN SOUFFLÉ
6 portions

- 4 eggs, separated
- 4 cups soya bean pulp
- 4 teaspoons minced onion
- 3 tablespoons minced parsley
- 1 1/4 teaspoons salt
- 1/8 teaspoon pepper

Beat egg yolks until thick and lemon colored. Add soya bean pulp, onion, parsley, salt and pepper. Beat egg whites until stiff but not dry; fold in. Pour into greased casserole. Bake in very moderate oven (325° F.) 40 minutes or until set.

SOYA BEAN TID-BITS

Soak soya beans overnight. Drain. Dry thoroughly. Fry a few at a time in shallow fat (1 1/2 inches deep) heated to 350° F. for 8-10 minutes. Drain on absorbent paper. Sprinkle with salt while hot. Serve with cocktails.

GREEN AND YELLOW VEGTABLES ...
FOR VITAMIN A

Are you eating at least one large serving of a yellow vegetable or a green vegetable every day? You should, you know, if you want to be sure of getting enough Vitamin A (especially now that several animal sources of this vitamin—liver, kidney, fat fish, butter, cream—are on the scarce or rationed lists).

Vitamin A is good for the eyes. If you get enough, you won't suffer from night blindness or "glare" blindness, because your eyes will react normally to changes in light intensity. Then, too, Vitamin A builds up resistance against infections of the breathing system (nose, throat and lungs). It is needed for strong bones and teeth. It prevents dry, rough skin and hair. And it aids appetite and digestion.

◇◇

Vitamin A is found abundantly in spinach, Swiss chard, dandelion greens, kale, romaine, lettuce, mustard greens, collards, broccoli, turnip greens, sweet potatoes, carrots, yams and winter squash. Green beans, green peas, green asparagus, green peppers, green lima beans, brussels sprouts and yellow corn, are good sources. (Just for your information, certain fruits are good sources, too—apricots especially, then yellow peaches, cantaloupe and oranges. So are tomatoes—but we come to those later in this book.)

Don't get in a cooking rut! Serve green and yellow vegetables in new and different ways. Switch from spinach to kale or collards, just for a change. Combine a green and yellow vegetable for vivid color accent. Cook carefully and season well. The following recipes will give you a good start.

GREEN PEAS AND SCALLIONS
6 portions

- 4 cups shelled peas
- 1 cup boiling water
- 1 bunch scallions, peeled
- 2 sprigs parsley
- 2 sprigs fresh chervil
- 1 teaspoon sugar
- Butter, salt and pepper

Drop peas into rapidly boiling water. Add scallions; parsley and chervil tied together; and sugar. Cook until peas are tender (15-20 minutes). The water should have cooked away. Remove parsley and chervil. Season to taste with butter, salt and pepper.

MINTED PEAS

Add a small bunch of fresh mint while peas are cooking. When peas are done, remove mint, season to taste with butter, salt and pepper. Sprinkle with a little chopped fresh mint.

GREEN BEANS LYONNAISE
6 portions

- 1 1/2 pounds green beans
- 2 medium onions
- 3 tablespoons butter
- salt and pepper
- minced parsley

Cook green beans in boiling salted water until tender (15-30 minutes). Drain (save liquid for use in soups or sauces). Slice onions thin, cook in butter until soft and yellow; add to beans. Season to taste with salt and pepper. Garnish with minced parsley.

CORN MEXICALI
6 portions

- 3 cups yellow corn, cut from cob
- 2 tablespoons butter
- 2 tablespoons chopped green pepper
- 2 tablespoons chopped pimiento
- 1/2 teaspoon salt
- 1 teaspoon chili powder
- 1/4 cup water

Heat corn in butter; add remaining ingredients. Simmer 10-15 minutes, stirring frequently.

VERMONT SWEET POTATOES
6 portions

- 6 medium sweet potatoes
- 1/3 cup hot milk
- 3 tablespoons butter
- 1/2 teaspoon salt
- dash of pepper
- dash of nutmeg
- 1 teaspoon grated orange rind
- 2 tablespoons melted butter
- 2 tablespoons maple syrup

Boil sweet potatoes; peel and mash. Add hot milk, butter, salt, pepper, nutmeg and orange rind. Beat until fluffy. Pile in baking dish. Top with melted butter and maple syrup, mixed. Bake in a moderate oven (350° F.) 25 minutes.

CARROTS IN BOUILLON
6 portions

- 2 medium onions, diced
- 2 tablespoons fat
- 12 carrots
- 1/4 cup flour
- 1 cup bouillon
- salt and pepper

Cook onions in fat 5 minutes. Slice carrots lengthwise, roll in flour; add to onions; cook until flour browns. Add bouillon. Simmer 1/2 hour. Season to taste with salt and pepper.

RING O' GREENS
6 portions

- 3 cups finely chopped cooked greens (kale, spinach, chard, etc.)
- 1 small onion, minced
- 2 tablespoons butter
- 1/2 cup soft bread crumbs

◇◇◇

- 2 cups thick white sauce
- 2 eggs, separated
- salt, pepper, paprika

Cook onion in butter 3 minutes. Remove from heat. Add greens, crumbs, white sauce, and slightly beaten egg yolks. Mix well. Season to taste. Fold in stiffly beaten egg whites. Turn into greased ring mold (for smaller recipe use individual ring molds), set in a pan of hot water and bake in a moderately hot oven (375° F.) 30 minutes or until firm. Unmold. Fill center with creamed chicken, eggs, left-over meat or vegetables.

LEAFY VEGETABLES PRIDE VITAMINS, IRON, BULK

We know that green, leafy vegetables are a splendid source of Vitamin A. Let's not forget that they supply us liberally with iron, too. Or that they keep the digestive system in good condition by supplying some of the bulk or "roughage" that we need every day.

Cooked, or served raw in salads, leafy vegetables ring the changes that give meals variety. Salads, you know, should be served the year 'round, not just during the summer. Some people like a salad for the first course, others for dessert, with crackers and cheese.

Try fresh, young spinach leaves as a salad green—nice for a change! Soup, plus a hearty salad and dessert make a good meal, whether the weather is hot or cold.

When you cook greens, cook them with imagination, don't just boil them and let it go at that.

To show you what we mean, here are some recipes, dedicated to good appetite and buoyant health.

SPINACH SOUFFLÉ
6 portions

- 3 eggs, separated
- 1/2 cup medium white sauce
- 1 teaspoon grated onion
- 1/2 cup grated American

cheddar cheese
- 2 cups finely chopped cooked spinach

Beat egg yolks until thick and lemon colored. Combine white sauce, onion and cheese. Stir egg yolks into white sauce mixture. Add spinach. Fold in stiffly beaten egg whites. Set in a pan of hot water and bake in a moderate oven (350° F.) about 50 minutes, or until firm.

DESSERT SALAD
6 portions

- 1 cup cubed oranges
- 1 cup diced cantaloupe
- 1 cup diced peaches
- 3 tablespoons powdered sugar
- 1 1/2 cups gingerale
- 1/4 cup lemon juice
- 1/4 cup finely chopped fresh mint
- Lettuce
- Watercress
- Mint sprigs

Combine fruits and sugar. Mix gingerale and lemon juice; pour over fruits. Chill 2 hours in refrigerator. Drain. Mix chopped mint with fruits: Serve on lettuce and watercress, garnished with sprigs of fresh mint, with French dressing sweetened with honey.

SWISS CHARD WITH CHEESE
6 portions

- 1 cup milk
- 1/2 pound American cheddar cheese, grated
- 1/2 teaspoon salt
- 1 teaspoon prepared mustard
- 4 cups cooked, finely chopped Swiss chard
- 1 cup bran flakes
- Butter or margarine

Combine milk and cheese; cook over hot water until cheese melts, stirring often. Add salt and mustard. Put chard in casserole; add cheese mixture. Top with bran flakes. Dot with butter or margarine. Bake in a moderate oven (350° F.) 30 minutes.

MIXED GREEN SALAD

Have greens chilled and crisp. Serve in a salad bowl with French dressing. The following combinations are quite special.
1. Romaine lettuce, watercress, chicory, sliced green pepper.
2. Raw spinach leaves, shredded lettuce, curly endive.
3. Lettuce, dandelion greens, watercress, sliced radishes.
4. Escarole, Boston lettuce, sliced scallions, green pepper rings.
5. Romaine lettuce, sliced cucumbers, chopped scallions.
6. Lettuce, watercress, sliced stuffed olives, diced cheese.

SALAD BOWL
6 portions

- 1 bunch watercress
- 1 bunch chicory
- 1 head lettuce
- 6 radishes, sliced
- 1 cup diced celery
- 1/2 cup thinly sliced raw carrot
- 3 tomatoes, diced
- 1 bunch scallions, chopped
- 1/2 cup crumbled blue cheese
- 1/2 cup French dressing

Break the crisp, chilled greens in small pieces; add remaining ingredients and mix very thoroughly. Serve in a salad bowl with additional French dressing.

KALE, RUSSIAN STYLE
6 portions

- 4 cups chopped, cooked kale
- 1/4 cup minced onion
- 1/2 cup sour cream
- 1/2 teaspoon salt
- few grains pepper
- dash paprika

Combine all ingredients; heat thoroughly.

BREAD AND CEREALS FOR ENERGY

There is good reason to call bread the staff of life, particularly now that popular white bread is enriched with B vitamins and iron. White flour, too, has been enriched. Insist on it, when you buy. Many favorite cereals have been "restored" with B vitamins and iron, so that they have the same food value as *whole grain* cereals, volume for volume.

Bread and cereals are energy foods ... they supply fuel for the body which creates the energy we need to carry on our work. In these strenuous times, the more energy, the better!

Best of all, there is no sign cf any shortage when it comes to cereal products. We still have the staff of life to lean on!

No shortage in variety, either. Ingenious manufacturers have provided us with a huge variety of ready-to-serve cereals, as well as the kinds that need cooking. These cereals can be used in recipes as well as for breakfast food ... and cereals and breads make grand meat extenders. Try these recipes and see.

CHEESE MUFFINS
6 portions

- 2 cups sifted, enriched flour
- 3 teaspoons baking powder
- 1/2 teaspoon salt
- 3 tablespoons sugar
- dash paprika
- 2/3 cup grated American

cheddar cheese
- 1 egg, well-beaten
- 1 cup milk
- 3 tablespoons shortening, melted

Mix and sift flour, baking powder, salt, sugar and paprika. Stir in cheese. Combine eggs, milk and shortening; add to flour mixture, stirring only enough to dampen dry ingredients. Fill greased muffin pans 2/3 full. Bake in a hot oven (425° F.) 20 - 30 minutes.

MOCK VEAL CUTLETS
6 portions

- 1 pound veal, ground
- 6 tablespoons fat
- 2 cups cooked rice
- 1 cup thick white sauce
- 6 stuffed olives, minced
- 1 teaspoon salt
- 1 egg, beaten
- 1 cup fine bread crumbs

Cook veal in 2 tablespoons fat until well browned (1 tablespoon for small recipe); mix with rice, white sauce, olives, salt and egg; cool. Form into cutlet shapes; roll in crumbs. Fry in remaining fat until lightly browned. Cover; cook slowly 10 minutes. Serve with tomato sauce.

BREAD PUDDING

Try cutting bread into small cubes instead of crumbling it. Then use the cubes in your favorite recipe. Different! Whole-wheat raisin bread makes super bread pudding No need to add more raisins.

CORNMEAL GRIDDLECAKES
6 portions

- 1 1/4 cups sifted enriched flour
- 3/4 cup cornmeal
- 1 teaspoon salt
- 1 tablespoon dark molasses
- 2 eggs, well-beaten
- 1 1/2 cups milk (scant)
- 2 tablespoons shortening,

melted

Mix and sift flour, cornmeal and salt. Combine molasses, eggs and milk; add to flour mixture slowly, beating until smooth. Add shortening. Bake on hot griddle.

BREAD CROUSTADES
(USE INSTEAD OF PATTY SHELLS)

Cut stale bread in 2 1/2 inch slices; remove crusts. Remove centers, leaving a shell about 1/2 inch thick. (Use crusts and centers for crumbs.) Brush with melted butter or margarine and bake in a moderate oven (350° F.) 15-20 minutes, or until golden brown. Fill with any creamed mixture.

CASSEROLE TOPPINGS

Any of the flaked, ready-to-serve cereals make fine casserole toppings. Mix 1 cup of flakes lightly with a little melted butter or margarine and sprinkle on casserole.

OATMEAL DROP COOKIES *(MAKES 36 COOKIES)*

- 1 cup sifted, enriched flour
- 1 teaspoon baking powder
- 1/2 teaspoon salt
- 1 1/2 cups rolled oats
- 1/2 cup seedless raisins

Mix and sift flour, baking powder and salt; stir in rolled oats and raisins. Stir brown sugar into egg; beat well. Beat; molasses, marmalade and shortening into egg mixture. Gradually stir in oatmeal mixture. Drop from teaspoon on lightly greased baking sheet. Bake in a moderately hot oven (375° F.) 12-15 minutes.

BRAN AND HONEY MUFFINS
6 portions

- 2 cups sifted enriched flour
- 4 teaspoons baking powder
- 1/2 teaspoon salt
- 2 cups bran
- 1/2 cup chopped walnuts
- 1 egg, well-beaten
- 1/2 cup honey
- 1 1/4 cups milk
- 1 tablespoon shortening, melted

Mix and sift flour, baking powder and salt; stir in bran and nuts. Combine egg, honey, milk and shortening; add to flour mixture, stirring only enough to dampen dry ingredients. Fill greased muffin pans 2/3 full. Bake in a hot oven (425° F.) 25 - 30 minutes.

CITRUS FRUITS AND TOMATOES . . . YOU NEED THEM EVERY DAY

Everyone has heard of Vitamin C. Nearly everyone associates it with a vague idea of scurvy. Few realize that without it teeth and gums suffer, nerves are jumpy and irritable, complexions look muddy, joints suffer from fleeting aches and pains, bruises appear too easily, appetite and digestion suffer, and resistance is lowered.

Furthermore, the harder we work the more Vitamin C we need. The body will not store this vitamin, so it is up to us to get enough every day to prevent all the symptoms listed above, and to assure us of vital good health. The surest way to get enough is to depend on oranges, grapefruit and tomatoes (fresh, cooked, or canned). All you need, each day, is one large orange, or 1/2 grapefruit, or 2 tomatoes, or 2/3 cup orange or grapefruit juice or 1 1/3 cups tomato juice. Easy, isn't it?

But if you get tired of these foods served just "as is," try them in the following recipes.

TOMATO ASPIC SALAD
6 portions

- 2 1/2 cups cooked or canned tomatoes
- 1 small bay leaf
- 1/2 teaspoon salt
- few grains cayenne
- 1/4 cup minced celery
- 1 tablespoon grated onion
- 1 tablespoon plain gelatine
- 1/4 cup cold water
- 1 tablespoon lemon juice
- Lettuce
- Mayonnaise

Cook tomatoes, bay leaf, salt, cayenne, celery and onion 10 minutes. Strain; reheat to boiling. Sprinkle gelatine on cold water; dissolve in hot tomato mixture. Add lemon juice. Pour into individual molds which have been rinsed in cold water. Chill until set. Unmold on lettuce. Garnish with mayonnaise.

TOMATO FRAPPÉ

Season tomato juice to taste with salt, pepper, Worcestershire sauce, prepared horseradish and sugar. Pour into freezing tray of automatic refrigerator. Freeze to a stiff mush. Beat vigorously with a fork. Serve at once, as a first course.

ORANGE FRUIT CUP
6 portions

- 2 cups diced orange sections
- 1 cup halved strawberries
- 1 cup white seedless grapes
- 1/2 cup orange juice
- Powdered sugar

Combine fruits and orange juice. Sweeten to taste. Chill. Garnish with sprigs of fresh mint

BAKED TOMATOES CREOLE
6 portions

- 6 medium tomatoes
- 1 green pepper, minced
- 1 medium onion, minced
- 4 tablespoons butter or margarine
- 2 tablespoons sugar
- 1 teaspoon salt
- 2 tablespoons flour
- 1 cup milk

Cut tomatoes in halves; place in shallow baking pan. Cook green pepper and onion in butter or margarine until onion is tender; add sugar and salt; pour over tomatoes. Bake in a moderate oven (350° F.) 20-25 minutes. Remove tomatoes. Add flour to mixture left in pan; blend. Add milk, cook until *thick*, stirring constantly. Pour over tomatoes.

GRAPEFRUIT MINT SALAD

Serve grapefruit sections on crisp lettuce, with French dressing to which chopped fresh mint has been added. Garnish with mint sprigs.

FLORIDA MILK SHAKE
6 portions

- 2 1/2 cups orange juice
- 1 1/2 cups grapefruit juice
- 1 cup evaporated milk
- 1 cup water
- 1/2 teaspoon salt
- 1/4 cup sugar
- 1 cup crushed ice
- nutmeg

Combine all ingredients, except nutmeg, in a shaker. Shake until well mixed. Pour into tall glasses. Top with a dash of nutmeg.

BROILED GRAPEFRUIT

Prepare grapefruit halves for serving. Pour off excess juice. Sprinkle with brown sugar and mace. Dot with butter or margarine. Broil 10 minutes or until delicately browned. Add juice that was poured off. Serve at once.

FRUIT SLAW
6 portions

- 3 cups shredded cabbage
- 1 cup diced orange sections
- 1 cup diced grapefruit sections
- 1 cup diced unpeeled red apples
- Cooked salad dressing

Combine cabbage and fruits. Add enough cooked salad dressing to hold ingredients together.

◇◇◇

MILK AND CHEESE . . . FOR CALCIUM

Everyone needs milk . . . and needs it every day, all their lives long. Milk, you see is the *only* food that supplies *calcium* in sufficient amount to meet the body's requirement. Then, too, milk is a perfect meat substitute as far as the quality of its protein is concerned, and it is rich in Vitamin B2 (riboflavin). To meet the demands of the body for calcium, children need a quart of milk a day, and adults need at least a pint. Fortunately for those who don't like milk as a beverage, milk can be *eaten* as custard, cream soup, pudding etc. Don't forget that unsweetened evaporated milk, plus an equal amount of water, has the same food value as pasteurized whole milk.

Cheese is concentrated milk. Hard cheese, of the cheddar type, supplies all the food value of milk. Ever since the war began to interfere with shipments of imported cheese, American manufacturers have been proving that they can make cheese every bit as good, and in just as great a variety. Get acquainted with these American-made cheeses — they'll lend a willing hand on meatless days, and add variety to meals all week long.

QUICK RICE PUDDING
6 portions

- 1 cup cooked rice
- 2 cups milk
- 2 eggs, separated
- 1/2 cup sugar
- 1/8 teaspoon salt
- 1/2 cup raisins
- 1 teaspoon vanilla

Combine rice and milk; heat over hot water. Beat egg yolks until thick and lemon colored; add sugar and salt. Add hot rice mixture slowly to egg yolks. Add raisins. Cook over hot water 5 minutes, stirring often, until thickened. Remove from heat; add vanilla. Fold in stiffly beaten egg whites. Chill. Sprinkle with nutmeg and serve with light cream.

SPICED HONEY CUSTARD
6 portions

- 1 quart milk
- 4 eggs, slightly beaten
- 1/2 cup honey
- 1/4 teaspoon salt
- 1/8 teaspoon cinnamon
- nutmeg

Scald milk. Combine eggs, honey, salt and cinnamon; add milk slowly, stirring constantly. Pour into custard cups; sprinkle with nutmeg. Set cups in a pan of warm water. Bake in a very moderate oven (325° F.) 1 hour or until inserted knife comes out clean.

To make a large custard, use 6 eggs (3 eggs in small recipe) and bake 1 hour and 15 minutes, or until inserted knife comes out clean.

CHEESE AND TOMATO SOUFFLÉ
6 portions

- 1 1/2 cups tomato juice
- 4 1/2 tablespoons quick-cooking tapioca
- 1 1/2 cups grated American
- cheddar cheese
- 1 1/2 teaspoons salt
- dash cayenne
- 1 tablespoon butter

- 4 large eggs, separated

Boil tomato juice and tapioca 1 minute, stirring constantly; add cheese, salt, cayenne and butter. Stir over low heat until cheese melts. Cool slightly. Stir in well-beaten egg yolks. Fold in stiffly beaten egg whites. Turn into greased casserole. Set in a pan of warm water. Bake in a moderate oven (350° F.) 50-60 minutes or until firm to touch.

HEARTY CHEESE RAREBIT
6 portions

- 1 pound American cheddar cheese, grated
- 1 tablespoon butter
- 1 cup beer
- 2 egg yolks, slightly beaten
- Hot buttered toast or crackers
- Paprika

Melt cheese and butter over hot water, slowly. When about 1/4 of the cheese has melted, add half the beer slowly. Continue to cook until cheese is all melted, stirring constantly. Stir remaining beer into egg yolks; add slowly to cheese mixture. Stir constantly until thick and smooth. Serve immediately on toast or crackers, garnished with paprika.

CHEESE-WALNUT CROQUETTES
6 portions

- 1 cup grated American cheddar cheese
- 1/4 teaspoon paprika
- 1 1/2 teaspoons grated onion
- 1 tablespoon minced parsley
- 2 cups thick white sauce
- 1/2 cup finely chopped walnuts
- fine dry bread crumbs

- 1 egg, slightly beaten
- 1 tablespoon water

Add cheese, paprika, onion and parsley to white sauce. Cook over low heat until cheese is melted. Stir in walnuts. Cool. Shape in cones or cylinders; roll in crumbs, dip in egg and water, mixed; roll in crumbs again. Fry in shallow fat (1 1/2 inches deep) heated to 380° F. about 1 minute or until golden brown. Serve with tomato or mushroom sauce.

DESSERTS THAPARE SUGAR

Americans love sweets, and in their estimation a meal without dessert is hardly a meal at all! Sugar-rationing or no sugar rationing, sweets there must be, and homemakers are meeting the challenge.

As a matter of fact, with molasses, corn syrup, honey and maple syrup at our disposal, we can't complain. Furthermore, we can use prepared pudding mixes, fruit flavored gelatins and semi-sweet chocolate in lots of interesting and delicious ways. The manufacture of ice cream has been curtailed, but we can make it at home, with the help of ice cream powders and recipes that call for a minimum of sugar.

We are sure you will want to add these recipes to your ever growing file of war-time desserts.

BUTTERSCOTCH SPANISH CREAM
6 portions

- 1 envelope (1 tablespoon) unflavored gelatine
- 2 1/2 cups milk
- 3 eggs, separated
- 3/4 cup dark corn syrup
- 1/4 teaspoon salt
- 2 tablespoons butter, melted
- 1 teaspoon vanilla flavoring

Soften gelatine in 1/4 cup of the cold milk. Beat egg yolks; add remaining milk, corn syrup and salt. Cook over hot water, stirring constantly, until like custard in consistency. Stir in melted butter. Add softened gelatine; stir until dissolved. Remove from heat; fold in vanilla and stiffly beaten egg whites. Turn into individual molds which have been rinsed in cold water. Chill until firm. (There will be a jelly on the bottom and fluffy custard on top.) Unmold. Serve with light cream.

CHOCOLATE CHIFFON PIE
6 portions

- 1 envelope (1 tablespoon) unflavored gelatine
- 1/4 cup cold water
- 1/2 of a 7-oz. package semi-sweet chocolate
- 1/2 cup water
- 1/4 teaspoon salt
- 4 eggs, separated
- 1/2 cup light corn syrup
- 1 teaspoon vanilla flavoring
- 1 baked pie shell

Soften gelatine in the cold water. Heat chocolate, remaining water and salt over hot water, until well blended. Beat egg yolks until thick and lemon colored. Add corn syrup; beat well. Add chocolate mixture slowly. Cook over hot water, stirring constantly, until of custard consistency. Add softened gelatine;

◇◇◇

stir until dissolved. Chill until mixture begins to thicken. Fold in stiffly beaten egg whites and vanilla. Turn into pie shell or tart shells; chill until firm.

CHERRY-GRAPEFRUIT PUDDING
6 portions

- 1 package cherry-flavored gelatin
- 1 1/2 cups hot water
- 1/2 cup grapefruit juice
- 1/2 cup diced grapefruit sections
- 1/2 cup pitted, halved fresh cherries
- 1/4 cup chopped walnuts

Dissolve gelatin in hot water. Add grapefruit juice. Chill until mixture begins to thicken. Fold in grapefruit, cherries and walnuts. Turn into individual molds which have been rinsed in cold water. Chill until firm. Unmold. Serve with gingersnaps.

HONEY TAPIOCA CREAM
6-8 portions

- 2 eggs, separated
- 4 cups milk
- 1/3 cup quick-cooking tapioca
- 1/2 cup honey
- 1/4 teaspoon salt
- 1 tablespoon grated orange rind

Mix egg yolks with a little of the milk. Add remaining milk, tapioca, honey and salt. Cook over rapidly boiling water 10-12 minutes. Beat egg whites just stiff enough to hold their shape. Fold hot tapioca mixture into egg whites. Fold in orange rind. Chill. (Mixture thickens as it chills.) Serve with light cream.

QUICK CHOCOLATE CREAM CAKE

Buy 3 sponge layers at the bakery. Prepare chocolate pudding mix as directed on the package, reducing milk to 1 2/3 cups. Cool. Spread between sponge layers. Place a lace paper doily on top of cake. Sift powdered sugar over the doily. Remove doily carefully.

CRÊPES SUZETTE

Make very thin pancakes, using prepared pancake mix. Spread with jam; roll up; dust with powdered sugar. Serve with the following sauce:

LEMON SAUCE
6 portions

- 3/4 cup light corn syrup
- 1 tablespoon cornstarch
- 1/4 teaspoon salt
- 1 cup boiling water
- 1 teaspoon grated lemon rind
- 3 tablespoons lemon juice
- 2 tablespoons butter

Add a little of the corn syrup to cornstarch; mix well. Add remaining corn syrup slowly, while stirring. Add salt. Gradually add boiling water. Bring to a boil; cook 15 minutes, stirring until sauce is thickened, and clear. Stir in lemon rind, lemon juice and butter. Stir until butter melts.

KEEPING A WHOLESOME HOME

One important help in the maintenance of sound health, in wartime, is a hygienically clean, well-ordered home.

With doctors so scarce, infectious disease — say health authorities — may be quick to spread, and may chalk up more casualties than War.

So fight *germs* . . . those hidden enemies of health . . . *by disinfecting as you clean* — with Lysol.

Whenever you clean floors, walls or woodwork, put Lysol disinfectant in your cleaning pail, as many leading hospitals do.

Used in cleaning water, Lysol gets *germs* as well as dirt. It has the power to kill every known germ of children's diseases and of typhoid, tuberculosis and diphtheria that may lurk, unseen, in your home.

Lysol makes cleaning easier, too. It's soapy in nature, helps remove stubborn stains. And Lysol costs little, because it's so concentrated — you dilute it with water as you use it, according to directions on the bottle.

LYSOL IN THE KITCHEN

LYSOL SOLUTION FOR CLEANING:

Use 2 1/2 tablespoonfuls of Lysol in 1 gallon of water.

KITCHEN SINKS AND DRAIN-BOARDS catch many germs. Help protect your family's food supply against the possibility of germ contamination. Disinfect with Lysol solution (directions above). Use this same powerful germ-killing solution for mopping floors, cleaning kitchen shelves and walls.

WHEREVER FOOD IS PREPARED and served, clean tables and trays with Lysol solution. Health authorities believe that many digestive ills, including dysentery, are spread by unsanitary methods of handling food. Help protect your loved ones. Use Lysol in the cleaning water. Won't harm paint or varnish.

GARBAGE PAILS BREED GERMS (germs easily carried by flies to food). Empty and clean garbage pail at least once a week with Lysol solution (above). Lysol deodorizes as it destroys dangerous germs. Its clean odor disappears soon after use.

LYSOL IN THE BATHROOM

DANGEROUS GERMS — including the fungus infection commonly called "Athlete's Foot"— may thrive in bathtubs and on bathroom floors and tiling. So clean all bathroom surfaces regularly with Lysol solutions. (2 1/2 tablespoonfuls to 1 gallon of water.)

THE TOILET SEAT — and Baby's toilet, too — are danger zones where germs may multiply. Disinfect with Lysol solution (same as above). Lysol is soapy in nature, helps remove stubborn stains, thus cleans more effectively. Makes things smell really clean!

FIRST AID for bruises, scratches, cuts. Whenever skin is broken, there is danger of infection. Wash injured skin without delay with Lysol solution. (Mix 2 teaspoonfuls of Lysol with 1 pint of water.) This germ-killing solution spreads when applied, reaches germs in crevices and skin folds.

LYSOL IN THE SICKROOM

LYSOL SOLUTION FOR SICKROOM CLEANING:

Use 2 1/2 tablespoonfuls of Lysol in 1 gallon of water.

WHEN SICKNESS COMES, help protect others of the family from catching the infection. Many hospitals use Lysol for this purpose. Wash all furniture, floors, woodwork with Lysol solution. (See above.) No harm results to paint or varnish.

EVERYTHING THE PATIENT USES should be washed in a germ-killing Lysol solution (above). As soon as they leave the sickroom, wash all china, glass, silver and trays. Also vessel used for bathing, bed pan or urinal. Even combs and brushes. Don't rely on "cleaning compounds," alone!

SICKROOM LAUNDRY may harbor virulent germs of infection Soak all patient's nightgowns or pyjamas, bed linens, tray linens, wash cloth, handkerchiefs, towels, overnight in Lysol solution (see above), before laundering. Lysol annihilates germs. Deodorizes, too.

Printed by BoD™in Norderstedt, Germany